Robert Johnstone was born in Belfast in 1951. He was educated at the Royal Belfast Academical Institution and the New University of Ulster. In 1973 he won the Walter Allen Prize for poetry, and in 1986 received an award from the Arts Council of Northern Ireland. From 1974 to 1986 he was associated with *Fortnight* magazine – as film and book critic and deputy editor – and he is currently co-editor of the *Honest Ulsterman*. His books include *Breakfast in a Bright Room* (Blackstaff Press, 1983), *Images of Belfast* (Blackstaff Press, 1983) and *All Shy Wildness* (Blackstaff Press, 1984). He now lives in London.

EDEN
to
EDENDERRY

ROBERT JOHNSTONE

THE
BLACKSTAFF
PRESS

BELFAST

First published in 1989 by
The Blackstaff Press Limited
3 Galway Park, Dundonald, Belfast BT16 0AN, Northern Ireland
with the assistance of
The Arts Council of Northern Ireland

Printed by The Guernsey Press Company Limited

British Library Cataloguing in Publication Data
Johnstone, Robert
Eden to Edenderry: poems
I. Title
821'.914

Library of Congress Cataloging-in-Publication Data
Johnstone, Robert, 1951–
Eden to Edenderry: poems/Robert Johnstone.
p.   cm.
I. Title.
PR6060.0434E3   1989   89-56
821'.914--dc 19   CIP

ISBN 0-85640-420-9

ACKNOWLEDGEMENTS

Some of these poems have appeared in the following: *Aquarius, Belfast Review, Belfast Telegraph, Fortnight, Gown, Irish Review, Krino, Linen Hall Review, North, Paris-Atlantic.*

'The constable's complaint' and 'The liberal's lament' were first published in *Fortnight*'s 'G.U.B.U.' column.

A selection was included in *Map-Makers' Colours*, edited by Todd Swift and Martin Mooney (Nu-Age Editions, Montreal, 1988).

Grateful acknowledgement is made to: Carcanet Press Limited and Houghton Mifflin Company for permission to quote from *The Sinking of the Titanic* (1981) by Hans Magnus Enzensberger; Cassell plc for permission to quote from *Brewer's Dictionary of Phrase and Fable*; the *Linen Hall Review*; and Padraig O'Malley for permission to quote from *The Uncivil Wars*, published by Blackstaff Press.

The author also gratefully acknowledges an award in 1986 by the Arts Council of Northern Ireland.

CONTENTS

III EDEN TO EDENDERRY

IV CHELSEA

I
TITANIC

I am trying to lift the lid,
logically, the lid
on my private crate.
It isn't a coffin by any means,
it is just a package, a cabin, or,
in a word, a crate.

from 'Security considerations'
The Sinking of the Titanic
Hans Magnus Enzensberger

ROBOT CAMERA

When they sent the robot camera down
into the unimaginably null
coldness and darkness of the Atlantic,
hoovering its floor with stadia of light,

and found the uncorroded *Titanic* there
waiting under that tonnage of water,
far down below its heaves and freaks, its clouds
of ice, noumenal, Babylonian,

when they beamed it back, blue-grey, on the box,
it was as if I was seven again,
bathing by the rocks at the Arcadia,
the time I nearly drowned in a breaker

and imagined I understood what death meant –
a breathless, weightless, infantile floating,
a rush of sound, an arm, my own, perhaps,
waving calmly in the mid-foreground

behind the motes and bubbles, sand and salt
particles, minuscule viscosities
migrating all over, aimless as me,
a five-pointed star tumbling in a wave –

how it was not unpleasant except when,
finding myself alive in air once more,
my chest cracked with the pain of the first breath,
the world looked hard, new-washed, indifferent,

compelling as that other silent film
of the whitey-blue, virginal liner,
which looked as if it might mean something more,
had been absorbed into the world of facts,

had made recognisable the face
of an object resembling my father
as the ship's captain, or rather his head
in wax on top of a stuffed uniform,

the expression stiff, the eyes like gross pearls,
saluting posterity for ever,
the third eye of his cap-badge still beaming,
balefully accusing me of life,

and in my nightmare the global current
irresistibly slips me near the wreck
as it remains in white rags of algae
waving on its intact surfaces like

the white hair of an old, honoured person,
and I could be a seal in my black skin,
I look through glass, drift in a bubble-swarm
till I penetrate the slit in the hull

to a space with crushed boxes spilling gold,
its sullen glowing the only life-spark
among the soggy ingots of linen,
a floating comb, tortoiseshell, a mirror,

depthless, colonised, a fountain pen,
then up the full-up, tilted corridors,
liquid as arteries, to the dead heart,
the ballroom, hollow, gaudy as a heart,

where the corpses of the revellers
twirl, bob and turn as perturbing water
jiggles them like a shoal of nervous fish,
fat bodies bursting from their finery

– a bosom overflowing décolletage,
a bull neck strangled by a thin bow tie,

a blimp with shirt-front flapping like a tongue –
then one ruined form floats towards me,

arms outstretched as if to take me dancing
somewhere between ceiling, floors and walls,
and when I push my hand goes through, right through
the tatters of its flesh, the chalky bone,

till it disintegrates in a cloudburst
of cloth and organic stuff comprising
the grey of mother-of-pearl as well as
patches of black and something reddish brown,

but instantly I see my hand swell,
the fingers inflate till the nails lift off,
my putty skin ballooning with a whoosh
and I'm floating again, disconnected,

like an infant, except I seem to know
which way is up, till I wake in a sweat
and reach out to touch the hardness of floor,
the carpet of silt from bed to dresser.

A SECOND DREAM

A second dream concerns how it might end
or, as I now believe, re-enter life.

In this one, the Atlantic Ocean's gone.

All the citizens make an excursion
to where their symbolism came to grief.

They circle the wreck, hurling out streamers
which bind their hands to their great creation.

It looks as if they've captured Gulliver.

The bands of the city play melodies
from Sousa, music-hall and ragtime,
ending with austere Miles Davis solos.

New World winds sandblast the heavy steel plates.

Bandsmen's instruments tarnish, fall silent.

Redness eats moth holes in thinning metal.

The ship collapses like a sheep carcass.

Before the pieces can bury themselves
people surge across the huge disaster.

They break up bits like bark and stamp them in
till a brown stain is all that remains.

The people return quietly to their homes.

The women's dresses, in thin materials,
are soiled and ripped, their naïve colours faded.

6

Bandsmen's jackets are undone. Braid hangs off them.

Once inside they strip off and burn their clothes.

No one is allowed any souvenirs
in this dream; grief is a personal thing.

I turn over and sleep easy in my bed.

WHEN IT SANK

When the grand vessel sank it slipped under
head first and must have plunged at an angle
downwards, tracing a glidepath of some miles
away from the crowded boats and those drowned,

those who would have been thrashing and gasping,
their lungs only purchasing on liquid
or, as they suffocated, all at once
going blissful and glad as the brain died.

As the embolus of icy water
advanced up the hull towards the boilers
there would have been some crumpling explosive
fizzle as fires drowned and steam supercooled,

a shuddering infarction, a big air bubble
maybe, that ballooned back up from the boat
and was seen, about to erupt, by the saved,
although already the ship would have gone,

sliding down the slope of heavy water,
leagues to the bottom, trailing behind it
silver bubbles, silver trays, cutlery,
bottles tumbling and twinkling like silver,

being gassy liquids in glass in water.

BUBBLES

How beautiful gases and bubbles are!
Really all our elements are liquid:
the smoke in plumes at the skirting board,
their curlicues liquid as oil in water
or ice in whiskey, or the fire itself,
a breath in the air, or fire in water. . .

Sometimes I liked to picture myself
within a cloud of oxygen bubbles,
floating airily about like Peter Pan.
I remember a plastic soldier trapped
under a bath tap, a sheet of paper
sucked up the chimney towards Santa Claus. . .

But it's also possible to imagine
submarine fountains, *jeux d'esprit* of pressure,
or a sheet of ash, letters black on black,
ascending over a bonfire, then lost
in winds and thermals, then just disappeared,
as all things dissipate ultimately. . .

We like things directional, connected –
Peter on his wire, the Reindeerland address –
when really things just move outward and die:
ripples in matter explain everything,
our being, our visions and our love.
Peter collides with the scenery,

the sheet of paper bearing my message
tumbles, folding and unfolding itself
like the hand of a temple dancer
or the elegant ballet of the leech
in the *Titanic*'s underwater wake,
a trail of starbreath down the frosty sky.

NOT AN EXPLOSION BUT A CRASH

It flooded from the bows and sank lower
till the ship pointed downward acutely
and then, of a sudden, something went crash
and all the innards slid forward and down:
the boilers and the turbine came adrift.
Its organs loose, the ship gutted itself.

Imagine, in sleep, you hear something –
wood splintering on the ground floor perhaps,
walls trembling after the Dublin express,
mattress trampolining in an earthquake.
As you leave the bedroom you hear a crash –
sounds like a ceiling's just collapsed downstairs,

except a hole's opening in the carpet,
a black bruise, and the furniture's falling –
so long, wicker chair, sofa, side table,
bookcase taking the rest of the carpet
and you, feet first, down through the storeys,
falling past lampshade and power cables

severed and graspless as arms panicking,
past beams, picture rail, wallpaper crinkling,
skirting board unpeeling, underlay
billowing in smoke virulent as ink,
so thick it might buoy you up like sparks
till you land, bump, on the bed of the fire.

The duvet slips off and all's madly clear:
you understand deathly cold; cold can burn:
but we can say it would have been instant,
the shock of the sudden plunge, breath-robbing,
an instant after the skittling from deck
of fearless tycoon, unlucky emigrant.

What's intriguing is that it could happen,
it could be you having that dream on board,
waking when the room shifted to the right
and the metal skeleton below groaned.
A sea monster, so you dreamed, turned over,
its belly made a shadow shape on sky.

More indifferent than a dumb animal,
the disaster wallowed at journey's end,
its upturned belly waterlogged and black.
You were roused from sleeping captaincy
of the soul voyage, your cruise of affluence,
steered by your own idea of the stars.

And – fancy meeting you here – it's a shock,
as always, when we bump together:
the charts were clear, but detail defeated us:
size had magnetised the ship to troubles;
berg and boat came close enough to make it
as inevitable as gravity.

UNDERTAKERS

It's disturbing that it's not a surprise,
to be drawn again towards that problem
lying down there so wonderfully whole
or scattered over the cold calm ocean.

Tonight I sail with the undertakers
out of a smudged newspaper photograph
of Halifax harbour, Nova Scotia.
We've ice, coffins, canvas, tools and chemicals.

The boys with the boat hooks keep plucking up
an awful number of hats, which they set
on deck like streaming molluscs – a top hat,
dunchers, one with ostrich feathers straggling.

A deckchair's now a door into water.
Three dead men in lifebelts lock together
like a snapshot of themselves dancing.
A woman still clings stiffly to a dog.

We identify, embalm, encoffin
all first-class passengers. Second and third
we wrap in canvas. Crew we pack in ice.
A question of time and money, drawing lines,

for even love, or grief, is relative.
Which reminds me – of the bodies laid out
at the Mayflower curling rink, visitors –
relatives – skidding from one to the next,

that poster of the unrecognisable
remains of a person mummified, it seemed,
in the fireblast of the hotel-bombing,
or the fireman gathering limbs in town,

the weeping priest waving his handkerchief,
a crowd of people walking, not running,
in ones and twos away from a cloud of dust.
Oddly, every one has her mouth open.

I dream there are no firemen to clean up
with bin liners. Walk down any street
and you could be in a necropolis,
Warsaw, Leningrad, some maiden city.

The starved or sick lie in their overcoats
like drunkards on the pavement. One walks by.
The van's stopped at the point it hit the child,
the child's body still lies where it landed.

A truck's still toppling a lamppost, a head
pokes through the windscreen, its face gone missing
like the shop front, blown inside out, rummaged
by a wind into an area of litter.

My mattress is a raft after the wreck,
it bumps through the bodies that bob like mines,
like balloons, like seals standing in water,
uttering their human, repentant cries.

I reach for a victim over the edge
but as my forearms submerge they dissolve,
I tip into the cushion of water,
erasing my face as I slip under.

I'm explaining how stupid this all is,
that I wanted to help, not be rescued,
but my words come out muffled in bubbles
and my lungs are filling like goldfish bags

when up rush two fast boats, one red, one white,
carrying the firemen and the nurse.

He takes his helmet off to look down at me,
she tells me softly to hold out my arms

(which I find I have) and I'm lifted up.
His big raw body kneels to shelter me,
her adolescent body shines with life.
She inoculates me with her selfless love.

IT CAN'T GO ON

Botanic Avenue, morning; drizzle.
Down the steps, at the door of the Empire,
under what used to be City Temple,
a bored bouncer's practising karate,
twisting-kicking and punching with stiff knuckles
the air two inches away from the bricks.

Brief Encounter's projected at the back,
its dialogue replaced by a jukebox.
There are playbills, old photographs, a glass case
of *Titanic* memorabilia.
Titanic chinaware, for example:
the great ship at the bottom of your soup.

No one's laughing, and no one seems disturbed
by the sex-crazed falsetto and pained guitars;
meanwhile in sweet England a train thunders
silently by the honourable wife
who's explaining to the handsome doctor
why they can't go on meeting like this.

OUTLINES

Sinking into sleep my body twitches
disconcertingly as though born again
or like men beside a car wriggling
as cops empty their weapons into them.

The corpse auras remain on the pavement
like fallen hardboards of figures dancing,
amoebae dividing, doing battle.
Each bullet's counted and circled with chalk.

Motes in my eye do a cellular reel
then turn into a fancy map of steps
and since this isn't real I follow them,
my feet can suddenly count to three.

But not for long. The disco lights expire,
the path of the machine gun and the foot
make strips of polka dots across the floor
and up a wall, the numbers don't make sense.

My eyes feel goggled, I swallow water,
a ludicrous fat man takes me dancing
through the drowned ballroom – shamed, asexual,
dandling in the swell of liquid darkness.

SOUTH KENSINGTON

after 'Charon' by Louis MacNeice

My hands are soiled with news and reek of money,
dirt from all the hands that held the coins.
I play with my magnetic ticket,
fold away the map whose folds wipe out
tracts of London like the bombers' tracks.

We stop, the doors sigh open, shut.
No one leaves or enters. An electric
pause till suddenly, with a thunderclap
like a train charging into a tunnel,
I know them all – they've followed me from home.

I expect them to shout *Happy birthday!*
or *Why don't you look like yourself? What changed?*
I'm on the wrong line, for the train lurches
what must be south, far under the river,
and someone explains, *You must pay the toll.*

You'll never get away with it. They cite
the victims on the burning stair, the man
they couldn't name, the mad, those seeking death,
old girls with plastic bags; they say, *Wise up,
face reality. Wipe that smirk off your bake.*

We stop, the doors sigh open, I get out.
They're wiped away, the strangers, into darkness.
I surface in the wake of tall museums
sailing through the clouds across the night,
my pocket full of coins with missing faces.

II
VERSES AND LOVE POEMS

When a god swore falsely by the Styx,
he was made to drink a draught of its water
which made him lie speechless for a year.

from *Brewer's Dictionary of Phrase and Fable*

THE CONSTABLE'S COMPLAINT

after 'A policeman's lot' by Gilbert and Sullivan

When an Orangeman's pursuing his enjoyment,
his enjoyment,
A-marching to his flute or bagpipe bands,
bagpipe bands,
He will tell you it's an innocent employment
'cent employment
Of time that would weigh heavy on his hands,
on his hands.
Oh, I like to see his banners all a-flutter
all a-flutter
And hear his flutes a-whistling very high,
oh so high,
But friend, my brains are not made out of butter
out of butter
And I don't like being in a fairground shy.

Oh,
When an Orangeman must march some other way,
other way,
He's as bad to policemen as the IRA,
IRA.

When an Orangeman's impressing Mrs Thatcher
Mrs Thatcher
And proving her Agreement cannot stick,
cannot stick,
He will chuck whatever missile that might catch her
that might catch her
Attention, from a bomb to half a brick,
half a brick.
He can't very well go blowing up Westminster,
up Westminster –
It would look bad, and Guy Fawkes was an RC,
an RC –

And he can't go shooting British Cabinet Ministers,
Cabinet Ministers,
So the only target is the RUC.

Oh,
When the British say he has to mend his ways,
mend his ways,
The Orangeman acts like the IRA,

IRA.

When loyalists appeal to their tradition
their tradition
And claim their critics sold out to the Pope,
to the Pope,
You can bet appeals to reason have no mission,
not a mission,
For their principles are permanent as soap,
just like soap.
They didn't mind our bullets made of plastic
made of plastic
When killing Catholic girls of ten or twelve,
ten or twelve,
But now their shock and outrage are fantastic
quite fantastic
When they find those bullets coming at themselves.

Oh,
When loyalists want policing to be fair,
to be fair,
They want the Micks to get the Orange share,
Orange share.

THE LIBERAL'S LAMENT

after 'Tit Willow' by Gilbert and Sullivan

On a stool in a bar-room an old Unionist
Sang, 'British, I'm British, I'm British.'
I said to him, 'Old man, why do you insist
You're British, you're British, you're British?
Does it come from an inferiority complex?
Or did you have problems in childhood with sex?'
He banged on the bar and he looked sorely vexed:
'I'm British, so British, so British.'

Jut then another appeared on the scene,
Singing, 'Ulster, I'm Ulster, I'm Ulster.'
And a man at the back, who was dressed all in green,
Said, 'I'm Irish, and Celtic, and Gaelic.'
I cried, 'Stop! For this whole thing could soon come to blows!
We none of us know who we are, and it shows.'
All three of them punched me, once each, on the nose,
One for Britain, one Ulster, one Ireland.

As I left I called out, 'Sure our family tree
Is part Scottish, part Irish, part English.
I don't give a toss about identity,
Whether Ulster, or Irish, or British.
For each of your gods I have only a curse!'
At this, the three of them looked fit to burst,
And they all then agreed that agnostics were worst,
Whether Ulster, or Irish, or British.

THE IRISH DISEASE

*My copy is literally coming apart as I write; so common is this
failing in paperbacks published in Ireland that I fear it may become
known as the 'Irish disease'.*

Gerry Healey
Linen Hall Review, vol. 2, no. 3

'Be gentle, it's my first time,'
thinks his latest fancy,
cracking a catastrophic smile.
New acquaintance is always chancy.

'She went to pieces in my hands,
halfway through she fell apart,'
the young critic complains;
'If she didn't mean it, why start?

'One after one, promising much,
they open up like flowers,
but, however gentle my touch,
petals drop in showers.'

An eager reader, soon ankle-deep
among the fallen leaves,
he rummages to pick them up
and reconstruct his splintered loves.

He peruses the pages again,
searching the initial savour:
'A dirty word and three puns
(although he's from impeccable Faber)

'suggest a consciousness like Muldoon.
Is this the iconoclast Foley,
with bodily functions and spoof jargon?
And could this be Mathews, or is it Sweeney?

'This is in dialect – Marshall or Paulin?
This must be Simmons, because it's rude.
And this could only be Medbh McGuckian:
I don't understand it, but I think it's good.'

In libraries and bedsitters
grow the snowy paper-drifts.
Like old flames the Irish writers,
Oliver Goldsmith, Gulliver Swift,

Patrick Kavanagh, Louis MacNeice,
Oscar Wilde and J.M. Synge,
lie together, lie at peace.
To the memorials readers bring

Mahon's shed, the bog of Heaney;
Poems of the Dispossessed,
every one a pleasant memory,
in the bundle with all the rest.

So let philanderers learn philology:
no sweetheart banned from the big anthology!

THE FUTURE OF LITERATURE

In the third decade of sound money
poets are released at last
from the prison of poetry.

They flood forth upon the world,
blinking in its harsh light
like sleepers newly waked.

One pats his pockets with inky fingers,
draws out a notebook,
puzzles, and puts it back.

How affecting to see them wonder
beneath the cherry blossom,
stammer at their girlfriend's door.

Their ears are cleansed of the iamb,
its numberless variations,
the nightingale holds no terror for them.

The poets are free to be rich:
one wants to be a photographer,
one has bought a guitar.

If they open their foxed collections
– with an indulgent smile –
the pages smell of indoors,

cigarettes and coffee,
the editor's desk,
dark shops, charity.

A VISIT

We change like the clouds in this temperate region.
They drift from the west steadily.
I could spend hours studying skies,
the sequence of clouds, the shapes they make,
what mood this piece of atmosphere's in.

I ought to be asking for information,
wheedling out your autobiography,
but we never put feelings in words.
The two of us normal, like sky,
aware of the colours, the forms and their reasons.

I never tire as they do what they do,
although I know where they're coming from,
and I think that we are like climate,
a direction prevailing, two tendencies.

THE PERSONALITY TEST

You play the *femme fatale* and then, with care,
set questions to select your new lover.

What I think of water's how I see sex,
the room we talk about is really death;

everything's a clue to the Real Me –
star signs, colours, the language of the body –

the way to the subconscious is metaphor:
you rattle the handle on that big door,

you wander in and out of the next room
(I left it open) and I ask your name

before we finally fall into bed.

We lie all night in a frozen embrace –
blank hours in a white room: one chaste kiss.

We cling and cling like the lonely and the dead.

LADY MACBETH

She had some problem with her sexuality.
Maybe that's what really turned me on.
That, and her insatiable fury
for sex in every possible position,

preferably in daylight, in the open.
I begin to put together reasons why –
her play-acting, power games, her sense of sin –
she had some problem with her sexuality

and every man and woman she would meet:
dominatrix and slave, pleasure in her pain.
She thought the same life ought to work for me,
and maybe that too really turned me on.

My career, a secret I wasn't in,
was to write romances, mystery stories
(her plots), for a killing on the book scene.
But, with her insatiable fury,

she left in clouds of homeless energy,
nearly gave up life till she gave up men
for girlfriends who'd rub off the memory
of sex in every possible position,

that itch of cells requiring surgery.
We can excuse what's understood; what's done
can't be erased: I still try eulogies
to loving her, again, again,
although she had some problem.

WE WERE WAITING

We were waiting for something to happen,
the phrase or the cadence that would make clear
what we meant to say, what the game was for.
To hear the truth, we kept our ears open.

Instead of telling we listened, like friends.
We took precautions against our growing
attached, promised outside ourselves, knowing
the messy way such stories usually end.

I knew our history before we touched,
your losses, our planned collaboration.
I saw with an authorial vision
what it would mean, when to give, and how much.

But the hands whose touches could teach us care
stayed idle, inarticulate with fear.

SESTINA

We broke each other's heart so many times,
and here we are, doing the same again:
I look with wonder on my childish crimes
and smile to think I lived through all that pain,
turning it to advantage in my rhymes:
I'd rather be your husband than Craig Raine.

You move off crying through the Belfast rain,
our kisses shortened by departure times:
I watch you through the drizzle on the pane
(another station witness to our crimes!)
and count your reappearance as a gain:
this present and the past make pleasant rhymes.

I feel that we are like a pair of rhymes,
I feel I've lived ten years upon your rein:
we seem to share the same view of our times,
the dream that soured, revolt become a pain,
the gentleness betrayed by tired old crimes,
the Tories back in office once again.

I sometimes think I'd like to try again –
I worried, maybe, too much at my rhymes –
I should have joined the fight against the reign
of capital, of pap, the *Sun* (*The Times*!),
the nuclear deterrent, and your pain:
complacency and hatred are bad crimes.

If history's mainly catalogues of crimes,
forgive me if I point out once again
how we were saved from everything those times
we were in love; and though it seems this rain
might make a nonsense of our parting rhymes,
our love can teach us how to deal with pain.

The tears we cry are not, I think, from pain:
as I review male-chauvinistic crimes
I hope I'm not as prone to them again
and want to take the struggle to my rhymes,
for now we have a garment against rain,
who broke each other's heart so many times.

How many times we caused each other pain!
But let us try again to salve our crimes.
Please take these rhymes out with you in the rain.

'FRIGID'

We must stop talking about having sex
the next time we get into bed:

it's rude, like talking about having fun
at every party we attend,

although most parties refer to themselves
and our wish to be together,

like last night's, when we, strangers,
told our lives and merely touched,

clothed in affection, though naked,
love being the way it's made.

A NEW AFFAIR

He said you ought to load each rift with ore;
each time you start you ought to act as if
making the inclusive, definitive
statement on everything that's happened so far.

But starting out gets more like sinking shafts
the straightest way towards that waiting ore;
side galleries take time that can't be spared
from mining's naked, sullen, headlong craft.

At the face you pick up fossils – no more
of history – you work with what you've got,
you slowly hack along the one-way street,
trying to remember what you're looking for.

Sometimes you pause and turn and look back out
to the people left at the shining door.

AN OATH BY THE STYX

One Indian summer
we made love in secret
by the double-Dutch of the river.

She never quite explained
her tears that final night.
We shivered in silence and watched

the moonlit, magnetic water.
So we escaped detection,
struck speechless for years.

This year in the mud
a plastic doll, a pram.
From lovers, maybe, upstream.

THE STEADY STATE THEORY

'Out there. Thattaway.'

Captain Kirk
Star Trek: The Motion Picture

This morning even the sun looks old.
Is it because you've gone to England?
How decadent are things in World's End?
In Belfast it's the end of the world.

I can't admit we're hurtling apart.
I prefer to imagine the sun
doing conjuring tricks with helium.
I want to be that big explosion,
envelop you in the final burn.
One thing might end: another can start.

Hoyle says life must constantly arise
out there, in the space between the stars,
where God's been hiding this hundred years,
where dreams go when we open our eyes.

THE BIG BANG THEORY

Should one think about more important things
than silk undies, the way you fill your clothes,
the tricks we play with fingers on ourselves,
the shape of an ear? Might there be meaning
underneath it all? Giant metal ears,
gramophones in reverse, are listening
for the littlest echo of the Big Bang:
the universe began, almost for sure,
like an orgasm, a split-second freedom,
when something couldn't take it any more.

We've made love like lovers for the first time.
(I whispered in your ear's canals, kissed the
resonating cave.) Now our nerves shiver,
each breath makes waves in the still of the room.

RADIUM

A picture from a book:
she stirred a vat
of seething clothes.

Her fingers raw,
she brushed hair off her temple
using the back of her hand,

paused by the cauldron,
fatigued as Marie Curie,

shook crystals of chemical
from a box coloured like sea.

The yard smoked like lava
when she flushed it clean.

Big sheets shifted
like doors on the line.

I moved in and out
of the corner of her eye.

If I fell, sure,
she could lift me still
with her hot, slippery hands,

she could give me the old hard soap,
then resume her experiments
with the bucket of blue steam.

A GLINT OF METAL

Open a drawer – metal glints.
Her room, the curtains drawn.
Gold spectacles in a shaft of sun.

In her absence, scent, the Empire chair,
a carpet where I saw an ancient, naïve
map of the world, predominantly red.

Her son and grandson dreamed
of oceans: she spoke of land and borders,
of buttermilk, oatmeal and the floury potato.

She drew a line at the foot of each order,
her eyes dazzled, ringed with gold,
she'd hair like documents, bleached linen.

Without her, sure enough, we lived in draughts,
the children left and Stormont fell.
White on the hill, it stands for her.

She gave us legends of smallpox and Famine,
white sheets of money, morocco, ivory,
the glisten of maple, walnut and oak.

I think of metals, gold and steel,
a plain ring, black gantries,
ships as great as Britain sliding down

when I open a drawer and find something
to ease the one-way trip. They explain so much,
syringe and crude needle, in their chrome box.

DIY

By my age you'd begun to gather things.
There was a rock with a pattern of moss:
we rolled it to the car and drove it home.
There was the door you never got round to hanging.

I like to think you're among such objects
one of those summer evenings
you claimed to be fixing something,
in a reverie on realness,

the creaky garage your paradigm
of how wood waits in sun and rain,
falling to bits as gradually as men,
how it swells and splits and whitens.

For twenty years of evenings
you observed the spreading of a rash
over an ammunition box,
fungal bloom on pigeon holes,

each with its stencilled number,
its chrysalis as jamjar,
abundant bolts of Yankee silk
melting into moth holes.

Now sun melts on our new gloss.
I would check my handiwork
with your brass-bound, folding rule,
your spirit-level's yellow eye.

DO YOU BELIEVE IN GHOSTS?

It was your love
in the doorway,
smiling with his open face,

whispering your name
so as not to wake you
over the bed.

He never sat still,
that's what you remember,
him standing up,

Sunday in the kitchen,
him at the low window,
admiring the crop.

You'd go for a walk:
how he could whistle!
He could charm the birds from the trees.

A ghost, you thought,
when he walked in his sleep –
alive without the spark of life –

made tea,
scanned the news inscrutably
and yet stayed asleep

as if he hadn't had time
or something had not been done
during the day.

That's how things are,
nothing's ever finished
while one of us remains.

You think of a fixed image,
him grinning like that photo,
but what you see's a gesture,

he walks out of a corner,
the words he mouths mean love,
their soundlessness fear.

Then you think he's like the spring,
permanent as land;
you see him stoop to look

but what haunts you's unexpectedly
the view itself from the low window –
a field waving like the sea.

III
EDEN TO EDENDERRY

A WALKING SHADOW

Cornmarket a dank clearing,
    a moving forest,
        umbrellas with legs.

Empire or Hippodrome.
    I sway on a tilted seat
        between Mum and Dad.

Men hide out in scenery
    but all's true and simple
        at the horse opera.

The Painted Desert's
    the waste ground
        behind Orpen Park.

When we leave the darkness
    I'm blindfold and surrounded
        by my classmates' ambush.

They throw down their branches,
    grown-up walking shadows,
        thickened, thin on top.

I walk out of shot.
    They hang round in dazzle,
        nodding at me like trees.

MUSIC AND MOVEMENT

His arms are branches,
his fingers twigs,
watch them shiver
in the wind.

When it's calm
we stalk through bushes
to pick an apple
from the bough.

The wall's all glass
and might well show
approaching water-
colour storms.

Back to class we creep
like the first amphibians,
effortfully, immensely,
everything to come possible.

As we get there
the first big
drops
fall.

THE PAROCHIAL HALL

No more self-improvement.

Instead of tying knots
I mitched off up a ladder,
opened a trap door into dust
and found things forgotten,

a lumber room of glamour:
there were cardboard rocks,
a slice of cottage wall,
a well of black shadow.

When *Jack and the Beanstalk* came
I'd learned it wasn't nice
to admire the Principal Boy,
her perfect legs in tights.

She moved like a flame in brilliance
and the hall was granted warmth.
There were jokes I couldn't unravel,
three wishes I couldn't recall.

THE FALL OF ROME

There was a Sunday school
where the children made a circle
round gentlemanly Mr Hall.

He held forth. He had chalk
and, to the kiddies' mute shock,
scrawled a cross on the table top.

The Boy Hero thinks someone –
cleaners or the Canon even –
must come upon that sign

when everybody's gone home
and wonder what was going on.
But now he's with Miss Brown

– *Stella* – things are more calm:
she sits telling them
a tale of father Abraham.

The Boy Hero imagines
a world filled with alarums:
the conversion of barbarians,

martyrdom, love, Stella,
or that dream of his father
cleaning a gun in the corner –

for sport and not for harm
although he fought the Hun.
Ten years on you find some

swastikas chalked on telegraph poles
by a fan of Hannibal,
pretend Visigoth or Vandal.

ME AS MOSES

That was me in the ark by the Nile;
it was for me the dark princess fell,
my northern colouring, my green eyes.

I could imagine a childhood in palaces
among bare-breasted servants,
wearing linen, my head shaved,

leading my people,
marching them through the sea,
making promises God would keep.

The force of my personality
would show my brother what to say.
They would remember me

pointing at hills and valleys,
pastures we'd never make home,
which we would never surrender.

EDEN SAYS NO

(graffito in Eden village, County Antrim)

As a people favoured by the Almighty,
we discovered writing for ourselves
(we've got our own historians, and poets –
some have dubbed us handy with a phrase).
Hence that slogan daubed on the Garden wall.

A reptilian representative
from a firm of nurserymen
(not one of us, if you catch my meaning)
tried to induce us to turn commercial
with free samples of edible fruit
and all types of honeyed talk.

But we know what we've got in Eden
and we aren't about to throw it away.
The slogan reminds us, as much as them,
that our soil must stay pure and unsullied.
Within these walls fruit shall never grow
because Eden will always say No.

SUPERGRASS

Budgie Allen as a child
repeated what you said.
Hence the name.

The women of his victims
dress as budgies on the street
outside Crumlin jail.

You can get lost in a story;
the cameraman enjoys himself
no less than the clown,

a joke, like this, can lose its way,
an amazing fact can live
by the hearth of a missing room.

When I see them on the box
I sketch my scenario,
in which I name names:

I would have them dressing up
in skin, fur and feathers,
parading beneath my window,

indignant at my lies,
my truths,
my loaded stories.

DOUBT

Drink had been taken the night he told us
what it's like to be raised a Catholic
– doubt like needles in Roman haystacks
to ex-Prods like us, in misalliance.

He left in a fret (had you run away?),
while you slept like Gretel in the spare room.
I woke you and took you in chilled pursuit,
and didn't admit I wished you would stay.

Even then the whole story seemed absurd.
But he wasn't far. We found him by three,
lurking like some wood-kerne under a tree,
the soft Irish rain spangling his curls.

AFTER TENNYSON

(The Lotos-Eaters)

One afternoon they came upon a land
in which it seemed perpetual afternoon
despite long shadows on the ribs of sand,
the evening star, the rising of the moon.
They took a cottage, settled in, and soon
life slowed down, the way the waves always break.
It was too much trouble to play a tune
on whistle and guitar, they didn't take
the time to plant, he didn't paint, she didn't bake.

Instead they watched the clouds drift from the west
and how the raindrops dripped in through the thatch
and how the values they had once professed
became bright schemes they knew would never hatch.
The dole bought lentils, roll-ups, and they'd catch
a fish or two; they wanted less and less.
The biggest industry was to darn and patch
their woolly socks, their jeans, her peasant dress:
the pictures in their minds required their idleness.

They wandered round with sleep still in their eyes,
the light in things, their looks, an alien pale,
they gave up speech, they lived in a disguise
of bliss until that bliss began to fail,
things turned aslant. They left that place where clouds sail
across a hill which always seemed the same
but changed momentarily. Their change entailed
our wider paranoia, and they came
back like frazzled dreamers into another game.

LIFE, THE UNIVERSE AND EVERYTHING

I've a friend who'd like to think
there's an answer to it all
which *they* are keeping from us.

An equation in a folder, say,
stamped TOP SECRET in red ink
and ONLY FOR YOUR EYES.

Once a month the President
presents his dual key
to white-gloved, dyslexic guards.

Or maybe a machine
under a tarpaulin
or shrink-wrap polythene

all alone in a huge hall
blistering a desert plain
where metal never rusts.

Or a wilderness in central Asia,
a square of wire and sentry towers,
floodlights saying 'Christmas' to the dark.

Or a damp Down in the Home Counties,
a jar in a prefab laboratory
and M.o.D. on the gate.

Mr Jones, waved through
in his Morris Minor,
almost late,

the windscreen steaming up,
bears, a silent hero,
his awesome responsibility.

WILD SIDE

You can appreciate
sentiment and threat
in the tartan Rangers waistcoat
framed on the wall.

*You can belong
just because of who you are.*

Take it in no bother:
a menu-board listing names
of the hunger-striking dead
and *Crown Court* projected
over the lunchtime drinkers.

The barmaid's on good form.
She cracks a dirty joke, sings
'D.I.V.O.R.C.E.'
just like Tammy Wynette.
She's bleached blonde and looks the part.

The bar's a pause
from the light of day.
Its dreams are brass, velvet, amber.
And it's real, it's real as chrome,
Formica and bar-room pool
and what we are being given now,
. . . *God made honky-tonk angels,*
and other things I didn't know.

THE LITTLE RED BOOK

Confused with dope or a day's sun at the City Hall,
she gave me someone's copy of The Little Red Book.
Light can blind you too, she said. She saw through everything.
I see her impossible sanity as monochrome television:
nuns inflicting pain, professors planting rice,
the burning monks, the marchers' style, the stony War
   Memorial.

She puts down the book. No, she's not content.
The crazy Christian gives her a cyclostyled message, magenta.
It's still here, tucked inside the plastic cover:

> *YOUR STORY HAS TOUCHED*
> *MY HEART*
> *Never before have I spoken to*
> *anyone with more troubles*
> *than you.*
> *Please accept this card*
> *as a token of my deepest Sympathy.*

A message printed twice. It's paper, it isn't card.
She's mortified. She giggles as he plies the winos
with sheaves of indiscriminate regard.

PROTESTANT BREAD

In Little India,
over the river from the Holy Land,
in the shadow of the bakery,
Brother J. stoned again.

Unusual to find him
at his interminable task,
scraping paint from the window frame,
slow as with a holy text.

Nights, clothes airing,
the ecological stove,
beans in the pressure cooker,
ecumenics, yogis,

brawls on the Ormeau Road,
Christians making noisy love
athletically upstairs,
The Who, The Grateful Dead.

Mornings, inch by inch,
when bare wood appears;
marijuana, incense,
poignant aromas of Protestant bread.

ALLOTMENT

Handy genitalia,
    pea pods display themselves.
Every stalk spirals
    like a molecular model.
Tendrils cling to stalks or,
    losing their aim,
coil in diminishing
    swirls of thread.
Where one tendril
    grips a pod
the plant hugs
    itself in error.

I'm picking peas on Gwyn's plot
    (my sister's husband
uses English
    to tell me how)
on holiday, a refugee
    from a climate of ideals
to earth's rich
    pragmatism,
the tourists' view,
    the spire on Ruthin's hill,
the alien picturesque
    of the Church-in-Wales.

A PHOTOGRAPH

Tommy Sweetlove signed the Covenant in his blood.
He was an ostler when the War
became the flu pandemic.

Every Sunday he'd walk four miles
to the Church of Ireland, Balmoral,
praise God and walk back.

The seasons on his way
reminded him of others –
summer's long sleep, lanes of clean snow.

On Christmas Eve he'd change
from donkey jacket to top hat:
Burlington Bertie from Bow.

I've a photo of Tommy
holding his favourite racing pigeon
gently like a child.

The expression on his face
could be enthusiasm
or shy, careful pride.

ADVICE

In one of the existences I contemplated for a second
my father, a lieutenant colonel, say (retired),
spoke to me on the veranda over his brandy-soda:
Son, you're starting in the world. I don't care what you do.
But take some advice from an old 'un. Life, in my experience, is
a bucket. We each begin with a certain amount,
and if you use up the water, you'll find the bucket's dry.

He wasn't a man normally given to extended metaphors.
In fact, that's the only one I remember. I was deeply
    impressed.
I occasionally picture those parents who put by their lives
    for later,
lounging in their easy chairs and looking out at vast distances,
for sundown's always theatrical there, behind the great tree:
the chirr of insects, apes' howls, bats like birds in a
    faraway panic,
a beast wailing in the night of Zambia, Zimbabwe, Malawi,
    Botswana.

ELEMENTS OF CRITICISM

You escape
by a road that clings to cliffs
in gales or sea mists
or the spotlight and sequins
and supercharged air
of the summer's heyday,
past every colour and consistency of rock,
as if to approach or leave
required a course in geology.

Or your mind's eye escapes
over hills creating a sunset
to prairies and deserts
where everything sparkles
and all the shadows are long.

Suddenly the air you breathe
is precious and endangered
and all you see is too real –
the separate grains of sand,
the particles of rock,
the individual blades of grass –
each unrepeatable furrow of bark
glows autonomously.

            *

When I think of it,
which I do more easily
when I'm somewhere else,
it's the name of a fish
washed up by evolution,
it's a shaft of sunlight
through a frosted window,
a glass of beer,
onto a walnut table,

it's a tone of voice,
it's bloodstained money bills
under the stones of stately buildings,
shells and wooden shillings baked in bricks
of alleys dragging their sick lives out
in pathetic darkness.

There's truth in abundance,
all kinds of truth,
so much that you want to run
to an uninhabited island
with your hands over your ears
and concentrate on necessities
– which fruits poison,
how to make a fire –
yet there nature is generous
and plays no nasty tricks;
you could, if you wanted,
sit in an orchard
– of which there are plenty –
and wait for the apples to fall,
secure in the knowledge
that everything's healthy:
you could, but of course you don't.

Also,
fire is as common there
as bricks or the air you breathe,
Greek fire tossed in a schoolboy arc
or the policy of scorched earth
when hills burn like metaphors
for the society of men
or the great ceremonial fires
when every movable scrap is scavenged
to make little mountains
hard by the houses
and torched on a certain night of the year.

They're used to playing with fire
and if it gets out of hand
they hardly seem to care,
they might leave the hillsides bald
and burn themselves from house and home
but that, they say, is just a regrettable
by-product of the ritual.

Fire might be the main element
of that complicated place,
except that, when I think of it,
all people and places
are made of the same things;
there's the liquid eyes
and the well-oiled tongue
and the land they chose to build on,
which can't decide if it's water or earth.

The igneous rock of native volcanoes
in fact overlays its opposite:
at the side of the path
on the edge of the plateau
strata are exposed,
invulnerable dark rock,
then the white of bones
that breaks up at your touch.

And the air is different too:
it's thick, it's overcrowded
with banners,
spires,
metal,
smoke,
there's a constant static,
prayers and bells,
mottoes,
curses,
cries and crashes.

When you're somewhere else
you hear the crash in the night
as a mere accident
– someone passed through crumbly glass,
flesh merged with metal:
there the bang occasionally
is not of coming together
but of flying apart. . .
I reflect that objects always
– cars in the street,
the hammer, the thumb –
tend to come together,
while it is very difficult
and involves a lot of planning,
noise and energy
to make things fly apart.

When you're somewhere else
all those words,
the prayers especially,
sound like babble;
they are so busy with words,
words heavy with meaning,
they speak in tongues,
but say their orotundities
in the thinner air up here
and they drop like lead balloons.

In spite of everything, I'd like to say
that just because something's wrong
doesn't mean it can't be right,
that language isn't a means
of telling the truth;
up here I'd like to curse
the tyranny of truths,
to suggest alternatives
in thought-bubble, mouth-music.

What it is when I'm away
is something out of reach,
something I can't get my tongue around,
a tone of voice,
a flag nailed to a pole
over a lonely farm,
a fish that evolved on its own
and was given a misleading name
where all names are disputed,
the spotlight and sequins
of the summer's heyday.

INSOMNIA

Tie, shirt and sweater,
sloughed off in one,
lie on the bedside chair.
Their empty heart remembers me.

Books loom round, arboreal.
Their paper hearts, the poet says,
yearn for wood, for innocence.
They think that I remember them.

Light grows into streets and rooms.
Does my head grow to their shape
or do the spires and trees conform
to the shape my day will take?

Above the city, a dome of light.
The clock ticks me into sleep.
I have some notion of a place
where things revert. I dream of flight.

AFTER *LEAVES OF GRASS*

Very well then, if you say so, we contain continents.
Antarctica, for instance, an upturned dish of snow,
two sets of footprints leading to the centre, one back.

Fringing the coast is a bit of old Europe,
a port of bungalows, terraces converted into flats,
a huge round library, a modernised museum.

But it's easier to talk in smaller terms:
the tree in the wild garden holds out its arms
to the constant wind that always flies away;

nights we hear it moaning as we settle round the box
to gaze at pictures of realer places – a red
emptiness, a wet maze in all the exotic greens,

or the plains of Asia, a possible descendant of the Khan
wrapped in many lengths of coloured cloth,
decorated carelessly with dagger and Kalashnikov.

Finally sophisticate, yearning for the serious romance
somewhere abroad, we invent new rituals
from images beamed in of the savage and the tribal.

One might be the warrior, one the slave musician.
The sacred river, the sunless sea, refer to our own bodies.
Honeydew might be a drug or the juice of intercourse,

suggesting our confusion about pleasure and desire
(piquant dreaming danger where nothing is forbidden).
Unwind my turban, see my long hair flow like water:

over the blank hinterland giant shadows play;
we are weaving circles, my hand is on your belly,
and our souls, our chemicals, seek each other blindly.

My fingers twitch like dowsers' rods over *Mare Nostrum*,
the legendary site of that warm and lovely sea,
which we came from, which we heard about, but which we
  never saw.

OCCASIONS OF LOVE

When I think to name
the occasions of love
I come to the death
of our neighbour's son,

Constable Mee, *mown down*
in a hail of bullets/
shot from a passing car/
claimed by the IRA

– the papers and my father
told their stories –
and if I were to film
the Great Ulster Movie

I would picture the gunman
stepping into a gunpowder mist,
backlit, feeling odd and tall
(like John Wayne, I'd hint),

striding across the wide pavement
to where the young lad lay,
a black bundle by our door
in his new, loose uniform,

and the gun would be cocked
and brought to his temple
and fired twice.
And fired twice.

But I would rather write
a novel about love:
Constable Mee on his home beat
nodding to his father's friends,

how we grow nostalgic
for an array of stores,
a society of Sabbath girls
in hats and pastel colours,

the common feeling of the folk,
how a body might join
one side or another
for a delicate reason.

It would have to end
with my return from England,
entering our house,
shutting out his final place,

his blood and brains
black and white
making a sign
on our front-door step.

LAST WILL

Odd that I obliged them
to execute my will:
did any of us once know
what my will was?

I've passed on when they come,
wondering was I like this,
without standards, with belief
in everything.

Surprised to find
'my own room' –
so small that any visitor
must rub against me.

Was this how I 'worked',
or translated my thoughts –
ideas starting on one sheet
to end elsewhere, in other words?

On paper we appear
capable of anything.
Because I'm not here
they can't ask what it means.

Not history in any large sense. . .
they feel awkward intruding,
but I wanted them
to sort out my death.

Beyond the window
there are special circumstances.
They light up and look round,
meaning no disrespect.

71

Beyond the window
are grass, trees, an interlocking fence,
and the place fills quickly with smoke,
so the light's filtered.

It flatters my oil of strangers
descending from hill cloud
to share their cults
with a farming people.

I've given the men
extravagant feathers,
the women smiles
and a confident stride.

The figures in black
exiting left
could be local clergy fleeing
their icons of pudenda.

And here, in a bundle,
billets-doux of the *affaire*
I'd like to have had
with the wife of my friend.

In this case real people
collaborated on a form of words
describing real feelings
transcended, which we then posted.

Only such phoney letters
embarrass them now;
the private papers – bills,
receipts, guarantees – are immaterial.

The heirs, whose faces
I can't imagine,

eye them and my testament
with suspicion.

Such bundles of passport photos,
each with four shots of my face,
each frame minutely different!
Are these all I left?

THE AFTERLIFE

As in a dream, something's eerily real
during Admissions visiting hour:
I'm the body in question, the poor Fool,
at somebody's wake, on the Bedlam tour.

During Admissions visiting hour
my friends crowd round in the tiny room:
they talk at the wake, on the Bedlam tour;
we're timeless yet real, like a hologram.

My friends crowd into the tiny room
to give their love and pay their respects,
though I'm just three dimensions, a hologram,
and they talk of the soul, not burns or cuts.

They give their love and pay their respects,
although my fingerprints have been erased:
they talk of the soul, not burns or cuts
although my face has been rearranged.

Although my fingerprints have been erased
I'm the body in question, the poor Fool;
although my face has been rearranged,
as in a dream, something's eerily real.

ROMEO C. TOOGOOD:
BARGE AT EDENDERRY 1936

(Acquired by John Hewitt for the Ulster Museum)

Is this picture of somewhere real
which appeared caught and pictorial,
glowing, as here, in a long light,
or is it less subtly lit
than faded, the roof of red iron,
the bluish sky, dulled in their planes?
Did the little wood's original
look smudgy yet oddly immobile?

Possibly the barge's hull,
curved huge and simple,
or the muscly bargee,
pausing rather too elegantly
(or posed, maybe, self-conscious),
suggesting the uncertainties of flesh,
those ventilators, or that off-white wall,
made the moment recognisable.

Did it look like a picture, an idyll
on the Lagan, or an interval
in the decade of Auden–MacNeice?
How was it made to look strained and ominous?
What would Hewitt have seen?
What does Toogood's joke mean,
flotsam bearing his signature
slipping by on the slack water?

AT THE END OF THE DAY

. . . invariably everyone was referring to the reckoning to come when the ledgers of hate would be balanced and the accounts of history finally settled. . .

Padraig O'Malley
The Uncivil Wars

Cars process past houses, all purchased
    on the never-never,
the sun drips gold on a pellucid
    blue evening of summer,
calm and full of threat, like the world's end,
    every car is silver
descending Tate's Bridge, each descendant
    tuned to the newscaster
– problems with traffic, X was blasted,
    man dead on his tractor,
and the news that what's been predicted
    has been proved true for sure:
the last trump will, or may, have sounded,
    there will be a free cure
for everyone who couldn't afford it
    and those caught in crossfire,
the bystanders, the unlucky dead,
    will learn that life is fair,
fire chariots will be seen overhead,
    the bricks will sag once more,
decisively, back to wobbly mud,
    we'll ask, 'What was it all for?'
except a tramp who loathes Jews, whose head
    is full of hate, desire
for wine, pain, who sinks back in fetid
    clothes, a sated lover:
'It was exciting while it lasted
    but I'm glad it's over.'

THE FRUIT OF KNOWLEDGE

In a wee, twee cul-de-sac
beside Kilroot
entitled the Garden of Eden,
a man on a kitchen chair
has placed himself in the sun
among grandchildren.

    The last image of my dad
    was in the rear-view mirror
    of the car he'd given me,
    my father and mother
    on the Lisburn Road,
    waving as I left for England.

But his hand raised
wishing good luck
also played an invisible line
to a fish tearing a hook:
in High Street now and Royal Avenue
I hear the waters under my feet.

    Someday, to release the world
    from the memory of what we were,
    the wave of the past,
    the wave of history,
    will drown grave, field and thoroughfare
    from the Garden of Eden to Edenderry.

IV
CHELSEA

A sonnet of sonnets

THAMES, RUN SLOW

Thames, run slow till you hear all my troubles:
no wood-kerne, an internal exile;
old soldiers attend at the Hospital
the river's transfusion of bubbles.

How foreign, those stanzas of Brodsky;
how homely the mud, the municipal lights:
imperial tastes which I recognise. . .
let's call this *To Moscow from Gorky*.

Across the river in the people's park
four golden Buddhas in a pagoda:
places are private in the Royal Borough,
the sculpture local to Cheyne Walk.

The disco boat passes cruisers and launches.
Dossers, crooks and the rich get free lunches.

PROBLEMS

Thames, run slow till you hear all my troubles,
give bargees a break from exporting refuse,
let the rich yachtsman postpone his travels,
hush the slide down the air of those jumbos;

tour guides can translate some folksy excuse
and tower builders cease from erecting,
factories and farmers must halt their abuse,
while the cops in their boat stop detecting;

let the refugees rest from defecting,
let fish, if any, take a breather at last:
though I find the whole scene so affecting,
as World and its cohabitee flow past,

I've problems of my own, I came with scars,
and would complain, but for the noise of cars.

THE MAN ON THE ULSTER NEWS

No wood-kerne, an internal exile,
the embarrassed, embarrassing cousin
you hoped not to see, who's 'just looking in'
but feels lost, like a tourist, a love child.

That might be him there in a wee while,
on thon bench: open-neck shirt, stubbly chin,
plastic bag, no socks, though it's cold as sin,
staring at the river with a dead smile.

I think of the man on the Ulster news
who carried his arm across several fields
and finally got it stitched on again.

I cursed my injuries and Irishness
in this very spot, long after they'd healed,
though I suffered surprise rather than pain.

ROYAL HOSPITAL

Old soldiers attend at the Hospital,
everything remaining proportionate,
like Wren's buildings, honoured, honourable.
They sit on benches and look. They hesitate,

remembering something, in the garden.
They carry their Safeway bags gingerly.
They sleep behind ornamental cannon,
faces gentler than the Oxfam ladies'.

They won their reward as professionals.
Their names are not carved on the stone lists.
They turn out for tacit photo calls,
quaint as King's Road punks to tourists.

The only Londoners who say hello
dream of Archangel, Dublin, Anzio.

THAMES BUBBLER

The river's transfusion of bubbles
is carried on in spite of everything.
A man on the deck watches life passing.
He yawns. The wake boils and the pump rumbles.

It reminds me of the lit-up cables
on the Albert Bridge (some bulbs are missing)
and the Big Top in the park, huge, looming:
somehow they're madly turning the tables.

Anoxia (or hyperventilation?)
makes you see things. I see England slip past
psychedelically: *Boy with a Dolphin*,
jumping catfish – nothing real, and the taste
questionable, while, given air, water, sun,
I imagine marshes, the Channel, the East.

'THE THAMES AT CHELSEA'

How foreign, those stanzas of Brodsky –
he must have been feeling lost and poor
to miss the charms of the Thames at Chelsea:
when you don't own a key and every door
is elegantly locked, you feel less free.

Round the black statue of Sir Thomas More
are assertions in gold – 'scholar' and 'saint':
he sits like stone on his statuesque chair,
peers out at nothing and hears no complaint
(the émigré asks what Utopia's for).

A heavy-set man who's close to my age
approaches from somewhere past Battersea:
Troops must break step says the sign by me;
his head shows first on the crest of the bridge.

LOYALTY

How homely the mud, the municipal lights. . .
Anything serves, given sentimentality,
even the fact that the Sea Cadets
hold their training on the hulk *Loyalty*.

The other night I dreamed I was heading
in the wrong direction, from west to east,
to a senior place where everything
was owned and worshipped as in the past.

It's unease at chained books in the Old Church,
the absence of hills, ghostly council towers,
money talking to trafficker and judge,
the sleeping shape in the open shelter.

If he and I are somehow going somewhere,
could we have imagined starting from here?

PAGEANT

Imperial tastes which I recognise. . .
the Embankment and Victorian lights,
cast-iron acanthus and Tudor rose,
fleur-de-lis, crown on the globe and claw feet.

Or a sexual joke I fail to get:
two wee boys climbing a Horn of Plenty,
the higher one waving the other's shorts.
(What did they think in the Beehive Foundry?)

Posing at every shop window in Chelsea,
pop stars, Tories, rich layabouts, tourists,
parade up and down in street comedy.
I find it odd that they share the same tastes.

We're actors 'resting', perfecting the art
of seeming to wait for the epic part.

SHORT-STORY WRITER

Let's call this *To Moscow from Gorky*.
A bumpkin blows in, a young hopeful
clutching reams of prose, to the capital.
His subject: growing up in the country.

The big river's comfortingly murky,
like the one at home, laden with black soil.
The critics find his work 'earthy and real'.
He settles in. He might join the Party.

To write you first must live, the proverb says,
and, no matter how pleasant the acclaim,
he grows to think there's a missing element.

He enjoys the city's chartered days
but prefers to watch the wide, muddy stream
drain away the substance of a continent.

STANDING FIGURES

Across the river in the people's park,
under the four-square chimneys, the real world:
a loving couple, he white and she black
either side of their beautiful brown child,

watching the deer in mating season.
Two bucks lock horns and shove for the high ground,
their maleness contest not beyond reason:
when the kid cries they both pause and look round.

Three Standing Figures, on a pedestal,
could be stalagmites or weathered rock,
but the simplified heads make it a vital
truth about how humans live, beyond talk.

Though loving is hard, we want to say yes,
to be part of the Sunday ordinariness.

DE PROFUNDIS

Four golden Buddhas in a pagoda
on the other bank, the southern hemisphere –
his enlightenment, on a lotus flower,
his passing away at Kushinara,

his birth, fully formed, in the Himalayas,
his first sermon – make four points of a star:
from Oscar's street I can look over there
and remind myself this life is *maya*

till I consult the key in my *A to Z,*
the villages of London scattered round;
there are more than two parts to any head,

we can be many things, profane, profound,
call to more than echoes, as the man said:
amongst the bird-song silent wind-bells sound.

BALANCE

Places are private in the Royal Borough
except to tradespeople and coloured maids.
The mad black scavenger's monstrous barrow
suggests property, like paper, degrades.

A house-warming party: settling in,
a couple anticipating burglars.
You can see through the house, every light's on,
every curtain back: at each window, bars.

When I envisage some personal place
I seem to start with a high balcony,
a viewpoint more than 'defensible space'.
Staring at the sky today, what did I see?

At a World's End tower, on a parapet
fourteen floors up, peering down, down, a cat.

CLOTHES

The sculpture local to Cheyne Walk
celebrates artists, tenants and their taste.
The Sage of Chelsea, seated, domestic,
in greatcoat, worrying about The Best;

More, his face gold, like some god of the East,
seated, fully clothed in hair shirt and ermine;
a *Boy David* to please the pederast;
then the naked, anonymous women.

Chelsea is where bondage became fashion,
the uniform of whores costume for the young.
Images remain in the confusion
and make weird sense to an outsider: one

is Thomas More, 'troublesome to heretics',
another's the shop they used to call 'Sex'.

LOUDSPEAKERS

The disco boat passes cruisers and launches,
a wobbly party burning on water,
thrumming from thought and teasing wishes,
a vulgar fancy outworking nature.

Between India (Battersea Bridge)
and Chelsea Bridge, thirties Egyptian,
the conspicuous in their blatant barge
sail to and fro: SS *Queen of Consumption*.

At dusk the Embankment's cheerier glow
reminds me of Ranelagh and Vauxhall:
dining pavilions, whoring in shadows,
Handel's music beneath the tinsel.

The pleasure boats look pleasant (let's be fair)
but none of them actually goes anywhere.

DESIGN

Dossers, crooks and the rich get free lunches.
Their stories somehow promise more weight
than those who work for a living, such as
the sick-eyed pop stars, dreadful in daylight,

the travel agent and the car valet,
clamp rescue, heroes of the service sector,
shop girls and the rest who model products,
showing off labels – or you and I – can offer.

Look around: at risk of exaggeration,
life's a con or a crime or a downer;
how much more tempting to make things happen
than be sold to, to get out from under.

Yet we go on, mostly, and merely say,
If we could choose, things would not be this way.

NOTES

pages 1–17 Some details are taken from *Titanic: Destination Disaster* by John P. Eaton and Charles A. Haas (PSL, Wellingborough, 1987).

page 57 'Little India' and the 'Holy Land' are areas in south Belfast.

page 85 *Thames Bubbler* is a boat which pumps oxygen into the Thames.
Boy with a Dolphin, a bronze by David Wynne, stands opposite the Albert Bridge.

page 86 'The Thames at Chelsea' is a poem by Joseph Brodsky.

page 87 Chelsea Old Church contains Thomas More's epitaph ('troublesome to heretics').

page 90 *Three Standing Figures* by Henry Moore is in Battersea Park.

page 91 Oscar Wilde and his family lived in Tite Street, from where the Peace Pagoda is now visible.

page 93 J.E. Boehm's sculpture of Thomas Carlyle, and Bainbridge Copnall's *The Boy David* are on the Embankment at Cheyne Walk.

OTHER POETRY TITLES

from

THE BLACKSTAFF PRESS

JESUS AND ANGELA
Paul Durcan

Paul Durcan's reputation as an exciting, highly original poet has developed rapidly in recent years with the publication of *The Selected Paul Durcan* (1982), *The Berlin Wall Café* (1985; Poetry Book Society Choice) and *Going Home to Russia* (1987). These three important titles are published by Blackstaff Press and are regularly reprinted to keep pace with the demand generated by Durcan's electrifying poetry readings in Ireland, Britain, Europe, America and Canada.

Many new fans, keen to read all of Durcan's work, have been unable to obtain some of his earlier titles. This book is the author's selection, with revisions, from work originally published in two separate books: *Jesus, Break His Fall* (1980) and *Jumping the Train Tracks with Angela* (1983).

198 x 129 mm; 112 pp; 0 85640 407 1; pb
£5.95

GOING HOME TO RUSSIA
Paul Durcan

'Paul Durcan's. . . collection is, as its title suggests, partly the record of a quest for a spiritual and imaginative home and a celebration of Russia, which the poet visited in 1983 and 1986. Directly and indirectly, the poems on this subject challenge patronising and complacent Western assumptions – both about Russia and the West – and raise questions about the nature of freedom. . .

'*Going Home to Russia* is a substantial collection, the work of an inventive and compassionate poet who continues to surprise and provoke and delight.'

Frank Ormsby, BBC Radio Ulster

'Any new work by Paul Durcan is to be hailed. He is a poet of such power, appeal and vitality that publication is to be eagerly anticipated. *Going Home to Russia* is no exception.'

Martin Booth, *Tribune*

198 x 129 mm; 112; pp; 0 85640 386 5; pb
£4.95

THE BERLIN WALL CAFÉ
Paul Durcan

This startlingly original collection, a Poetry Book Society Choice, sold out its first and second prints at breakneck speed and generated unstinted praise from the critics:

'The tenderness, honesty, imaginative daring at work, the generous, passionate personality which permeates the book, make *The Berlin Wall Café* the most riveting and moving collection of poems I have read for some time.'

Belfast Telegraph

'. . . a marvellous collection. There is nothing fragile, exotic or skybrained about this writing: it has heart and strength, and works in the world we know.'

Irish News

'What's finally moving in a poem is. . . the channelled pressure of something being said, the felt knowledge that this is a poem which had to be written. Paul Durcan's poems bristle with that pressure.'

Irish Times

Poetry Book Society Choice

198 x 129 mm; 80 pp; 0 85640 348 2; pb
£4.95

THE SELECTED PAUL DURCAN
edited by
EDNA LONGLEY

When *The Selected Paul Durcan* first appeared in 1982 the critics celebrated a unique talent: 'strikingly original. . . a poet to be reckoned with' (*British Book News*); 'Durcan's irreverent and iconoclastic vision is a liberating force in contemporary Ireland' (*Irish University Review*); '[he is] exciting and adventurous. . . as well as being a writer of real integrity and vision' (*Auditorium*, BBC); 'he resuscitates one's flagging belief in "the-poet-in-the-world"' (*Belfast Review*).

Poetry Ireland 1982 Winter Choice

198 x 129 mm; 144 pp; 0 85640 354 7; pb
£4.95

THE LONG EMBRACE
Twentieth-century Irish Love Poems
edited by
FRANK ORMSBY

Tender, passionate, bitter, bawdy, reverential – the poetry of love in Ireland is as various as the lovers and the poets. This anthology presents the best Irish love poems of the twentieth century. Some are uninhibitedly direct, others careful and emotionally circumspect but together they display the sturdiness, the fragility, the transforming power of love in its everyday, familiar settings and circumstances: love as it flourishes – or fails to flourish – in youth and old age, inside and outside marriage; love as a sharing of caresses, love ending in blows; love in time of war; love as it is trammelled by and defies the puritanical dictates of church and state.

Vigorously colloquial or musically formal, rich in imagery or quietly restrained, these poems, selected by the Irish poet Frank Ormsby,

> '. . . record love's mystery without claptrap,
> Snatch out of time the passionate transitory.'

'a very lively and accomplished collection'
Times Literary Supplement

'Every faithful spouse, every licentious rake, every heart-smitten or heart-broken lover should have a copy, preferably on the bedside locker.'
Irish Times

198 x 129 mm; 208 pp; 0 85640 387 3; pb
£6.95

ALL SHY WILDNESS
edited by
ROBERT JOHNSTONE

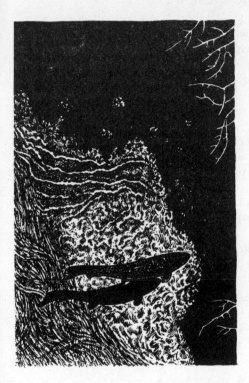

THE TROUT

John Montague

Flat on the bank I parted
Rushes to ease my hands
In the water without a ripple
And tilt them slowly downstream
To where he lay, light as a leaf,
In his fluid sensual dream.

Bodiless lord of creation
I hung briefly above him
Savouring my own absence
Senses expanding in the slow
Motion, the photographic calm
That grows before action.

As the curve of my hands
Swung under his body
He surged, with visible pleasure.
I was so preternaturally close
I could count every stipple
But still cast no shadow, until

The two palms crossed in a cage
Under the lightly pulsing gills.
Then (entering my own enlarged
Shape, which rode on the water)
I gripped. To this day I can
Taste his terror on my hands.

This enchanting anthology presents Irish poems about animals, birds and insects, by poets ranging from an anonymous eighth-century monk to Yeats and Heaney. A gift edition, limited to five hundred copies, quarter-bound in cloth, with matching slipcase.

Illustrated by Diana Oxlade.

198 x 129 mm; 84 pp; illus; 0 85640 322 9

£15.00